# THE

# ENTREPRENEUR'S

# BUSINESS

# ENVIRONMENT

# AND

# RISK MANAGEMENT

# APPROACH

## SOLOMON OKUSIRIKI

## DEDICATION

THIS WORK IS DEDICATED TO ALL WHO DESIRE A GREAT FUTURE THROUGH ENTREPRENEURSHIP. TO YOUR SUCCESS

## ACKNOWLEDGEMENT

My special thanks go to my wife and children for their support.

I appreciate my colleagues at work for their encouragement.

Most of all, my special thanks goes to the Almighty God for his wisdom and grace that are available to me.

# TABLE OF CONTENTS

# INTRODUCTION

Businesses do not exist in a vacuum, they operate in environments. An understanding of the business environment is vital in taking the decision to venture into entrepreneurship. The business environment determines the risks that the various businesses established in that environment will face. The environment also plays a huge role in the success or failure of the businesses. Since entrepreneurs are in business to make profits and continue in business while meeting identified needs of their respective customers, they should make it a point of duty to understand their environment of operation, the various risks inherent in their business environment and the various risk management strategies and systems that can be employed to mitigate the effects of those risks in order to ensure the continuous existence and survival of their businesses.

This book attempts to help entrepreneurs understand their business environment, identify and understand the various risks in their business environments, the implications of such risks if not handled appropriately and the steps and systems they can employ in dealing with the risks in their business environments accordingly.

# CHAPTER 1

## UNDERSTAND THE BUSINESS ENVIRONMENT

Businessdictionary.com defines business environment as "the combination of internal and external factors that influence a company's operating situation. The business environment can include such factors as: clients and suppliers; its competition and owners; improvements in technology; laws and government activities; and market, social and economic trends."

Entrepreneurs have the duty of understanding both the internal factors and external factors that can affect the continuity and survival of their businesses. Inherent in these factors are the various risks that can affect the profitability and continuous existence and operation of the business. It is therefore imperative that these internal and external factors are properly analyzed and quantified to appreciate the probable risks these factors can have on your business.

**INTERNAL FACTORS**

These are factors that are within the control of the owners and managers of the business that influence and affect the operations of the business. These factors can be grouped into:

- Objectives of the business
- The organization's corporate policies
- The business' information management system
- The composition of the management and board of the organization
- The organization's management style
- The organizational structure
- The corporate culture

**Objectives of the Business**

The objectives of the business define the reasons the business was set up in the first place. They point every stakeholder to what the business intends to achieve within a time frame. They are set up by the entrepreneur himself who defines the direction of his business. For every objective set, there are related risks either in the strategies employed towards achieving that objective or in the stakeholders' understanding of the business objectives. Those risks should not be overlooked. There is also the possibility of having stakeholders whose personal objectives are not completely congruent with the business objectives.

The entrepreneur should ensure that a common understanding of the business objectives as well as the related risks is established by continuous education of all stakeholders on the objectives of the business.

## The Organization's Corporate Policies

Investorwords.com defines corporate policy as "a formal declaration of the guiding principles and procedures by which a company will operate typically established by its board of directors or a senior management policy committee. Imbedded in corporate policy are the company's mission statement, objectives and the principles by which strategic decisions are to be made. It also forms the basis for measuring performance and ensuring accountability at all levels of the company."

The risks here involve the possibility of making the wrong strategic decisions; a stakeholder deliberately flouting the organization's guiding principles for whatever personal interests, etc. Business owners and the board of directors can decide to establish penalties for stakeholders who deliberately flout established guiding principles and procedures in a bid to ensure complete adherence to established guidelines.

## The Composition of Management and Board

The success or failure of any business can be directly connected to the composition of its Management and Board of Directors. Business owners should be careful on who makes the list of their Management team and Board of Directors. There is the risk of appointing people that are not suited for the type of business or who do not understand the business environment where the business operate into Management positions or even the Board of Directors. The composition of the Management and Board definitely affects the operations of the business. Business owners must therefore, ensure that their

Management teams and Board members are made of individuals with sound knowledge and interest in their type of business as doing otherwise could be detrimental to the profitability and continuous existence of the business.

## The Organization's Management Style

The management style adopted by the entrepreneur has a direct bearing on the speed with which decisions are made, the attitude of employees to the work environment and their respective roles, and ultimately on the achievement of set goals and objectives. An autocratic management style that does not give room for questions will get the job done either with the right attitude or with disgruntled staff. A disgruntled staff is a risk to the organization.

A democratic management style on the other hand, takes the view of all stakeholders into consideration by involving them in decision making. Stakeholders are satisfied with their jobs and the quality of work improves even though the process of decision making is slowed down.

Business owners must decide the best Management style that suits their businesses as no particular style in best for all businesses.

## The Organizational Structure

The organizational structure defines how people and their jobs are arranged within the organization. It spells out the tasks to be performed, as well as the coordination and supervision of those tasks towards the achievement of set objectives. The structure determines how the organization operates and as such affects the outcome of the organization's activities. Managements should ensure that the right individuals with the right skill sets occupy the right boxes in the organization's structure to avert the possible risks of having the wrong people in the wrong positions.

## The Corporate Culture

Culture is said to be the way of life of a people. It involves the language, belief system, music, dressing, etc. It defines the totality of the way of life of the people.

Therefore, corporate culture can be seen as the totality of the norms, characteristics and behaviors that all stakeholders of the organization, especially employees and management, are expected to imbibe in the conduct of their business.

The organization's corporate culture will be reflected in its dress code, working hours, employee benefits, hiring decisions, treatment of customers and every other aspect of the organization's operations.

The corporate culture should be one of the first things stakeholders, especially employees, should be introduced to in their first contact with the organization as it defines the way of life in the conduct of the business of the organization.

## EXTERNAL FACTORS

External factors that affect a business refer to those factors that are outside the control of the business owners. These factors can be grouped into the following:

- Political and legal factors
- Economic factors
- Social factors

- Technological factors

**Political and Legal Factors**

The political and legal environment is very important in the conduct of any business as it determines the boundaries within which businesses must operate. This environment deals with the various regulations that apply to the running of the various businesses in that environment. Entrepreneurs should therefore, ensure to be abreast with all government regulations that affect businesses generally and those that were enacted specifically for the industries where their businesses belong. It won't be a nice thing to start a business only to realize that you are in breach of the regulations set up for your type of business. Aspiring entrepreneurs should do enough research to get themselves fully abreast with all the regulations that apply to their businesses. Every entrepreneur should ensure they are always kept informed of new regulations and amendments to existing regulations.

INHERENT IN POLITICAL AND LEGAL FACTORS ARE THE POLITICAL RISKS BUSINESSES FACE.

**Economic Factors**

These factors are both macro and micro in nature. The macro factors affect the totality of the economy. Entrepreneurs should be concerned with issues like the prevailing interest rates, the current exchange rates of various currencies, the fluctuations in exchange rates, the economic trend of the business environment it operates, etc. These will help the entrepreneurs in decision making.

The micro factors on the other hand are specific to individual business types. They include the market size, demand, supply, relationship with suppliers and customers, distribution channels, and the number and strength of competitors.

**Social Factors**

These factors are related to the general society and relationships that affect and influence the business. Included here are social groups and their consumption behaviors, changes in fashion and consumption patterns, etc.

INHERENT IN ECONOMIC AND SOCIAL FACTORS ARE ISSUES LIKE EXCHANGE RATE RISKS, SUPPLY CHAIN RISKS, COMPETITION RISKS, MARKET RISKS, ETC.

**Technological Factors**

These factors are related to changes in technology. In this age of fast-paced technological changes and advancements, entrepreneurs must be interested and keep themselves constantly abreast with the various technological changes that affect various types of businesses. Such changes have the potential of either hurting or improving the businesses and as such, should not be taken for granted. INHERENT HERE ARE TECHNOLOGY RISKS.

## CHAPTER 2

## WHY RISK MANAGEMENT?

### *THE CHILD WORLD STORY*

*The Child World Corporation was founded in 1970. Its products included toys, electronics, board games dolls and video games.*

*The corporation once had 182 stores and annual revenues approximating $830 million.*

*Child World was the second largest toy retailer in the United States after Toys "R" Us, who were their chief competitor.*

*In 1981, Cole National Corporation acquired Child World together with the chain of business controlled by Child world.*

*While Child World focused its attention on building its brand, a recession that started in 1990 and continued into 1991, combined with a lack of "must have" toys helped to send Child World into a steady decline.*

*Peter Hayes and a large portion of Child World's Executives were fired in 1990 and Cole National started restricting capital to the store. As a result, Child World was unable to procure their needed merchandise for the upcoming holiday season and sales dropped. These led to a default in their payments to suppliers and creditors. The suppliers responded by refusing to accept orders for merchandise from Child World whose store shelves were becoming empty as suppliers were unwilling to do business with them.*

*The corporation recorded an annual loss of $192 million in 1990. The corporation's woes were then compounded by Toys "R" Us's continued growth, as well as the chain being named a co-defendant in a lawsuit* *filed by the Consumer Products Safety Commission.*

*In 1992, the store closures began. Child World closed 26 stores and exited certain markets altogether in January. It was later forced into bankruptcy in April after its line of credit was not renewed.*

*In 1992, Child world went public with its bankruptcy filling and announced 54 more closures leaving it with fewer than half of the stores that they had started the year with.*

*After a failed attempt at getting a new line of credit, Child World was left with two options: to either merge with another toy store chain to continue in business or liquidate and cease operations.*

*In July, 1992, Child World started selling off most of their inventory in order to raise cash. First, it was meant to be a massive chainwide clearance sale at its remaining seventy-one locations. On July 12, Child World announced that the clearance sale was being converted to a liquidation sale. On August 3, the company announced that the merger talks were unsuccessful. Within two to six weeks, liquidation sales were concluded and Child World stores were shut forever.*

Child World was obviously faced with major risks ranging from social risk to financial risk to competition risk to market risk; all of which led to their eventual collapse.

Entrepreneurs' need to be aware of the risks they could face in the course of running their businesses and setting up the necessary risk management systems to handle such risks cannot be overemphasized.

Risk Management systems are developed and employed not just to identify and analyze risks but to also help in determining the steps to be taken in ameliorating the effects of such risks. Before we continue, it is important to define what risks really represent.

## RISK DEFINED

Risk is an uncertain event or condition that, if it occurs, has an effect on at least one objective of the organization or business. It involves an exposure to the possibility of an unpleasant occurrence arising from the occurrence of the risk event. It might lead to a loss of profit, loss of customers, and injury to the business or a threat to the continuous existence of the business as in the case of Child World above.

Risk Management is actually the entrepreneur's proactive move towards prevention or reduction of the effects of risk events as and when they occur. What marks out an extraordinary entrepreneur is the ability to take proactive steps (rather than being reactive to happenings) to prevent or effectively handle the occurrence of risky events and situations.

Entrepreneurs must therefore employ risk management systems for the following reasons:

- To identify the risks the business is likely to face
- Analyze these risks
- Set up systems to either eliminate the risk or ameliorate the effect of such risk occurrences

In addition to the above reasons, an effective risk management system is likely to -

- Protect your invested capital
- Reduce cost of operation and wastages

- Reduce fraud and increase profitability
- Focus the entire Management team and employees on doing the right thing at all times
- Ensure safety standards are always employed in the running of your business
- Ensure effective use of resources
- Prevent and/or reduce distractions
- Keep the business focused on its key objectives

The entrepreneur must realize that inherent in every business opportunity presented to him are accompanying risks. Therefore, if businesses must expand by taking advantage of the opportunities presented, the entrepreneur must make risk management a major consideration.

Also, where suppliers are involved, there will be the need to consider the various supply chain risks the business could be exposed to and systems to handle them developed.

An effective risk management system will help identify and support the attainment of full potentials as an entrepreneur. Entrepreneurs must realize that the cost that will be incurred in setting up an effective risk management system will help save the organization when the risk is prevented. Effective risk management systems will help in identifying and analyzing the business' strength, weaknesses, opportunities and threats.

# CHAPTER 3

## UNDERSTANDING RISK MANAGEMENT

### RISK MANAGEMENT DEFINED

Investopedia.com defines Risk Management as "the process of identification, analysis and either acceptance or mitigation of uncertainty in investment decision-making. Essentially, risk management occurs anytime an investor or fund manager analyzes and attempts to quantify the potential for losses in an investment and then takes the appropriate action (or inaction) given their investment objectives and risk tolerance."

The above definition underscores the importance of risk management to the entrepreneur (investor). Entrepreneurs should consider setting up risk management systems when writing their business plans.

Businessdictionary.com defines risk management as "the identification, analysis, assessment, control, and avoidance, minimization, or elimination of unacceptable risks. An organization may use risk assumption, risk avoidance, risk retention, risk transfer, or any other strategy (or a combination of strategies) in proper management of future events."

We can pick out the following components from the above definitions:

- Risk identification
- Risk analysis
- Risk assessment
- Risk acceptance
- Risk avoidance
- Risk control/Mitigation of the effects of risk occurrences
- Risk retention
- Risk transfer
- Risk elimination

- Risk management considerations affects investment decisions

The above components will be discussed under the following headings:

1. Risk identification
2. Risk assessment/analysis
3. Risk treatment
4. Monitoring and continuous improvement of the chosen risk treatment option(s).

## RISK IDENTIFICATION

In identifying the risks any business could be faced with, the Entrepreneur must ask and objectively answer the following questions:

1. Where do risks emanate from?
2. What are the factors or events or behaviors that can lead to risky occurrences?

**Where do risks emanate from?**

Risks emanate from both internal and external sources.

Internal sources include the stakeholders of the business, the objectives of the business, the operational procedure/processes of the business, the management style of the business, etc.

External risk sources includes the political/legal environment of operation, changes in technology, changes in interest rates, exchange rate fluctuations, etc.

The entrepreneur must brainstorm along the lines internal and external risk sources to ensure the identification of as many risks as possible that the business is likely to face. In this process, do not overlook any risk, no matter how small they may appear. Small risks can become really costly as they have the potential of ruining the business.

The end product of this identification process is the production of a **risk register**.

The risk register is a register where all the risks identified by the entrepreneur and his team (where applicable) are documented and classified.

The risk register so developed is not meant to be a final product. It must be constantly updated as more risks are identified in the course of your operations. Risk identification therefore, continues throughout the life of the business if the business must continue to exist and succeed.

## RISK ASSESSMENT/ANALYSIS

This involves objectively evaluating the risks that have been identified in terms of the effects they can have on both the profitability and reputation of the business, prioritizing the risks and deciding on the approach to handling the risks.

Here, the entrepreneur must seek to understand how the identified risks can occur, where they can occur, when they are likely to occur, why they are likely to occur and the effects they are likely to have on the business.

Risk assessment, like identification, should be continuous and not one-off.

## RISK TREATMENT

The entrepreneur must decide on how to handle the risks that have been identified and analyzed. The following treatment options or a combination of the options are possible:

1. Risk avoidance

2. Risk acceptance

3. Risk control/mitigation

## Risk Avoidance

This involves avoiding the risk completely. Here, the entrepreneur may decide not to start that business at all, avoid taking advantage of an expansion opportunity, etc. The disadvantage here is that the entrepreneur will lose out on all the gains that come with taking advantage of the opportunities presented. Realize that not taking a risk is risky in itself.

## Risk Acceptance

Risk acceptance can be adopted by the entrepreneur when the risk identified and analyzed is not adequate enough to warrant the additional cost it will take to avoid or control that risk. The cost of managing the risk is therefore, accepted by the entrepreneur. The entrepreneur will do nothing about the risk until it occurs. Fixing these risks when they occur will cost less than to manage them. The risks that should be treated here are insignificant and of low severity.

### Risk Control/Mitigation

This is the proactive measure employed by the entrepreneur to manage, reduce and/or eliminate the risks that have been identified and analyzed. Methods of risk control include

1. Risk reduction
2. Risk transfer
3. Risk retention

#### Risk Reduction
This is meant to either reduce or totally eliminate losses that could have been incurred in the event of

the occurrence of such risk events. Examples of risk reduction measures the entrepreneur can employ include the installation of smoke detectors and sprinklers meant to quickly alert safety officers of a fire incident and reduce the damage the fire incident could cost the business.

**Risk Transfer**

The entrepreneur could also transfer the risk to a third party by insuring the risk with an insurance company. He can transfer part of the risk by placing a limit on the sum insured (value of the asset/risk insured) or insuring the entire asset at risk.

The entrepreneur can insure an asset that is at risk (building, vehicles, employees, operational equipments, etc.) or take out a business interruption policy that deals with risky situations that have the potential of interrupting the business' operations. Risks can also be transferred by way of contract to Third Parties, suppliers etc.

## Risk Retention

The entrepreneur could also adopt the captive insurance system. If you have the resources, you could set up your own insurance company that will insure your own risks alone. If not, you could start by setting up a sinking fund to enable you replace the assets affected in the event of the occurrence of the risk event or sustain the business in the event of a business interruption.

There are certain factors the entrepreneur must deal with in deciding to either transfer or retain the risk. Some of these factors include:

1. The transfer cost i.e. the premium to be paid
2. The financial strength of the insurer
3. The entrepreneurs' financial strength
4. Statutory and legal requirements

**The Transfer Cost**

The entrepreneur should consider the most cost effective means of controlling risks since he is in business to make profit. However, he must not sacrifice effective risk control on the altar of cost saving as it might be costlier if the risk event occurs. That said, the entrepreneur must ask himself if he is willing to pay the required premium to transfer the risk adequately or not.

## The Financial Strength of the Insurer

The entrepreneur must also do a due diligence to confirm the financial strength of the insurer before transferring the risk accordingly. He must convince himself that the insurance company he chose to transfer the risk to is financially buoyant enough to settle any claim arising from the occurrence of the risk event.

## Statutory and Legal Requirements

The entrepreneur must also consider statutory requirements in deciding either to retain or transfer the risk. This is because there are certain risks or businesses that are statutorily required to be insured. Therefore, he must ask himself if the law permits him to retain or transfer such risks or parts of his business risks before making the decision to either retain or transfer the risk.

## RISK MONITORING AND IMPROVEMENT

Risk monitoring involves a continuous assessment of the risk control measure adopted and implemented, continuous review of its effectiveness in relation to your business environment, and recommendations of improvements to the risk management strategy implemented.

Basically, risk monitoring and improvement involves the following:

1. Systematically tracking the risks that were identified
2. Continuously identifying new risks
3. Continuously evaluating the risk control measure that was adopted and implemented
4. Noting lessons learnt for future risk assessment and control efforts

The risk monitoring and improvement process must continue throughout the life of the business and must remain dynamic. It must respond to changes in the business environment to remain valid and effective. This is because new risks will always emerge while existing risks may disappear. Therefore, the risk monitoring process must be constantly updated.

Changes in the business' risk profile (i.e. the evaluation of the risks faced by the business and the acceptable risk limits) could result from changes and/or modifications to the business, business objectives, and other internal factors.

Such changes to the risk profile can also result from changes in the external business environment which could be political, economical, social or technological.

**Effective Monitoring and Improvement**

1. Set timelines for ensuring that identified risks are promptly treated.

Make sure the most urgent risks are treated first.

2. Write down when things need to be checked and tick them off the risk register as soon as they are checked. Also make a note of when the checked areas need to be reviewed again.

3. Keep records of incidents, accidents and near-misses and investigations into their causes. This will help prevent re-occurrences.

4. Be consistent with the type of records kept. It will be nice to have a specific form for keeping different kind of information

5. The records should also include regular reviews of the effectiveness of the risk management system employed.

6. Ask questions like
    a. How effective is our risk management system?

b. Is the measure employed working as expected?

c. How accurate is the risk assessment process?

d. Do we have a safer business because of the risk management system employed?

e. Are safety policies and procedure being consistently followed?

f. Are safety records accurate, consistent and up to date?

7. Ensure to set a feedback mechanism that encourages continuous identification and handling of new risks.

# CHAPTER 4

## SETTING UP A RISK MANAGEMENT SYSTEM

An understanding of the importance of risk management systems to the entrepreneur's business will be useless if the entrepreneur do not take steps towards setting up and implementing an appropriate risk management system for his organization. This chapter will therefore, provide a step by step approach to setting up an effective risk management system.

Our discussion will be structured under the following steps:

1. The Entrepreneur to define and establish the business' Risk Management Objectives
2. The Entrepreneur to identify and group the various risks according to functions

3. The Entrepreneur to assign the various risk groups to various individuals
4. Identify and select the most appropriate approach to handling the risks
5. Implement the most appropriate approach.
6. Establish a risk communication/feedback mechanism
7. Establish a system for continuous risk identification and analysis

**The Entrepreneur's Risk Management Objective**

Entrepreneurs must state clearly all their risk management objectives. It is very important to avoid ambiguity as much as possible. A clearly defined risk management objective will help all your employees understand the direction of the business in handling the various risks they are likely to face in the conduct of their various activities.

It is important to note that the risk management objectives must be derived from the overall objective of the business and must complement the business objectives. There must be no conflict in objectives.

In setting these objectives, the entrepreneur must also set the risk tolerance limits of the business to serve as a major guide to all members of the business. Everybody must be aware of their limits in taking any risk on behalf of the business.

Make sure the objectives are realistic and achievable.

## Identify and Group Risks According to Functions

Get all departments within the business to carry out brainstorming sessions to identify as many risks as possible that they are likely to face in carrying out their functions. Here, no risk should be viewed as being small. All risk identified must be documented and subjected to further analysis.

All risk identified and analyzed should be grouped and prioritized. This will help the entrepreneur know what risk group should be handled first and the treatment to be given to each group.

An understanding of the entrepreneur's business environment discussed earlier is vital in identifying and grouping the business risks.

Identified risks can be grouped by function and grouped further into **predictable** and **unpredictable** risks.

Predictable and unpredictable risks can be further grouped into "not severe", "less severe", "severe" and "very severe".

These groupings will assist the entrepreneur in deciding on what risk to ignore, what risk to retain, and what risk to outsource.

**Assign Risk Groups to Individuals**

The various risk groups should be made the responsibility of the various functional heads to which the risk groups relate.

The risk groups should not be left unattended to but should be assigned to responsible executive officers who will ensure continuous identification, analysis and control of all identified risks.

The persons to whom the various risk groups are assigned are to ensure that the risk treatment options adopted are effective and adequate, and make recommendations for improvements as the need arises.

## Identify and Select the Most appropriate Risk Treatment Option(s)

Having identified and grouped the risks according to functions, the next step is to identify and select the most appropriate option or options for handling the various risks. Here, the entrepreneur decides to retain, insure or ignore the risk or group of risks identified.

## Implement the Risk Treatment Option(s) Selected

Implement the selected risk management strategy or option.

If the entrepreneur chooses to retain the risk, he should immediately set up a sinking fund that will be sufficient enough to restore the business back to the position it was before the occurrence of the risk event or loss.

If he chooses to insure your risks, he should ensure the insurance company selected is financially sound and stable enough to cover the risk he is transferring to them. The Entrepreneur must carry out a proper due diligence to ensure the right insurer is selected. Here, the entrepreneur can look through the annual statement of accounts of the companies, speak to current and former customers of the company and ask about the claims payment history of the company among other things.

Also, the entrepreneur must ensure continuous review of all risk prevention measures adopted for effectiveness and further improvement. He must also keep himself continuously updated and open for better risk treatment options.

**Establish a Risk Communication/Feedback Mechanism**

The Entrepreneur must ensure the establishment of an effective risk communication and feedback mechanism; both top-down and bottom-up. A mechanism that ensures all identified risk and treatment options are communicated easily and quickly.

The risk communication mechanism should include the following:

- Preparation: This will deal with pre-occurrence risk communication which should outline the preparations made towards possible occurrence of identified risk events, including education on likely risk features of various threats.

- Response (Imminent Warnings): Also establish a mechanism that ensures crisis communication and guidance with respect to expected actions to be taken immediately prior to, in the midst of, or during the hours immediately following the occurrence of a risk event.

- Recovery: The Entrepreneur must also ensure the establishment of a mechanism that ensures the communication of messages regarding needs and guidance in the weeks, months, and years following the occurrence of a risk event.

Effective risk communication requires understanding where all the parties concerned are coming from in order to convince them to prepare better for risks.

## Establish a System for Continuous Risk Identification and Analysis

Every entrepreneur must understand that risk identification and analysis is a continuous process and this must be communicated to every member of the organization. Make sure to have a system in place that encourages the continuous identification and analysis of risks in your business environment.

# CHAPTER 5

## RISK MANAGEMENT CASE STUDIES

The book will not be complete without some risk management case studies aimed at propelling the entrepreneur into action. This chapter will therefore take a look at some case studies of successfully implemented risk management systems.

### Kenya Red Cross, Kenya – Risk approach

The Kenya Red Cross Society (KRCS) is the largest local humanitarian organization in Kenya whose core mandate is to alleviate human suffering brought on by disasters, disease and other humanitarian emergencies. The mission of KRCS is to be accountable to society through focusing its own talents and its partners' resources to alleviate the human suffering brought on by HIV/AIDS. KRCS is committed to delivering the highest standard of services to partners and beneficiaries as its contribution to a world free of the burden of AIDS.

As a Global Fund PR (Principal Recipient), KRCS supports the implementation of HIV/AIDS programmes aligned to the country's National AIDS Strategic Plan. This includes provision of anti-retroviral treatment (ART), prevention of mother-to-child transmission of HIV, HIV testing and counselling, interventions to support most-at-risk-populations, and provision of post-exposure prophylaxis. This also includes community systems strengthening interventions, capacity-building, and strategic partnerships.

Overall, KRCS defines risk at both strategy and operational levels.

Strategic risks include

- The possibility of irrelevance of its mission;

- Inability to reach its beneficiaries; and loss of partner support leading to failure to achieve its objectives and obligations.

Operational level risks include

- Loss resulting from inadequate or failed internal processes, people, and systems or from external events.

The KRCS risk management process involves three steps:

- identification,

- prioritization, and

- implementation of mitigating measures.

KRCS main ongoing risks, at both strategic and operational levels, involve its systems and processes for managing grant making to SRs (Sub-recipients) and other implementers. The organization applied risk management measures in its selection process for 51 SRs. Despite this, numerous risks arose related to weaknesses in governance and oversight, finance and contractual compliance, stakeholder engagement and transparency, in addition to low technical capacity to implement the programmes for which these organizations were contracted. In some instances, there was outright fraud or abandonment of contract leading to grant termination.

Based on these experiences, KRCS has instituted a number of risk management and risk mitigation activities, including training and mentoring in all aspects of programme development and implementation, including financial management, Monitoring and Evaluation (M&E), and training on technical competencies such as programming for key populations. It has also developed standard tools and guidelines to be used by all SRs and has instituted minimum requirements for equipment and human resources in order to deliver grant funded programmes. Through its regional structures, KRCS provides ongoing supportive supervision, requires monthly reporting and conducts reviews and site visits on a quarterly basis.

*To-date, some of KRCS' more successful risk mitigation interventions include*

- *close monitoring of the financial activities of SRs in order to track absorption and stewardship;*

- *actively engaging SRs in risk management by focusing on opportunities more than challenges;*

- *strengthening contractual agreements with SRs; and*

- *through targeting of capacity-building, coaching and mentoring to those SRs most in need of support.*

**EIFDDA, Ethiopia - Risk Management applied to OVC program**

The Ethiopian Interfaith Forum for Development, Dialogue and Action (EIFDDA) is a faith-based network organization that, as a PR (Principal Recipient), began implementing a 5-year Global Fund programme targeting orphans and vulnerable children (OVC) in 2009. The main objective of the programme is to enhance community ownership and response to HIV/AIDS through reaching about 20 million people by 2013 with community conversation and other means, and mobilizing local communities to support over 200,000 OVCs. In addition to providing holistic support to 350,000 OVC per year, the programme also seeks to build the capacity of EIFDDA and its members through a range of community system strengthening interventions.

To implement the grant, EIFDDA works with 9 SRs that collectively support 103 faith-based organizations working at community level. The main risks that have arisen during implementation and the risk mitigation activities EIFDDA has undertaken are shown in the table below:

**EIFDDA risk management strategies**

| Risks | How Risks are Mitigated |
|---|---|
| Inadequate M&E and data quality • Non-standardized tools at SR level. • Differential interpretation of | • Strengthen quality of supervision (supervisory checklist) & Increase Salary to retain Staff • Streamline and strengthen program performance monitoring |

| indicators at lower levels. | • Engage with HAPCO and USAID (largest contributor to OVC program) to ensure synergy and complementarity of support, and plan for transition through the National OVC Task Force |
|---|---|
| • Scale of OVC support under the current grant insufficient to make impact. | • UNAIDS and World Learning Training on Monitoring and Evaluation Software |

| Financial Reporting | • Adopt Quick-books Accounting software and conduct trainings on software to improve financial reporting |
|---|---|
| • Sub-optimal capacity among SRs | |
| • Weak institutional framework (all SRs are Board member) | • Internal auditor employed and making regular follow-up and audit activity on PR and SRs financial management issues |
| • Sub-optimal internal control capacity | • Improve PR/SR Grant Agreements for performance based funding agreements |
| • Weak monitoring from GMU (Grant Management Unit) | • Streamline and strengthen financial monitoring through a Financial Monitoring Plan approved at the board of EIFDDA (among all SRs) |

Going forward, EIFDDA will be enhancing its risk management capacities by engaging an independent audit firm to conduct annual audits at the PR and SR levels. The recommendations arising from these audits will be embedded in program agreements. EIFDDA will also work with the Country Coordinating Mechanism (CCM) to improve the quality and comprehensiveness of its reporting to, in turn, strengthen CCM oversight of grant implementation. Finally, EIFDDA will continue to strengthen and expand its supportive supervision activities at SR and community levels.

**AngloGold Ashanti Malaria Control Ltd, Ghana – Risk approach from the private sector**

AngloGold Ashanti (AGA) is a global gold mining company and the world's third largest gold producer. Headquartered in Johannesburg, South Africa, AGA has 20 operations on four continents. In Ghana,

AngloGold Ashanti operates the Obuasi and Iduapriem mines located in the Ashanti and Western regions respectively.

In 2005, the Obuasi Mine Hospital (Edwin Cade) recorded on average 6,800 malaria cases each month. Of these, 2,500 were mine employees. With an average of three days off per worker, an estimated 7,500 man-shifts were lost per month. This coupled with the slow work rate during recuperation, resulted in a major loss in production. The cost of medication for malaria treatment was USD 660,000 per annum.

In 2008, the Global Fund approved a total grant amount of $133million to scale up Internal Revenue Service (IRS) into 40 districts in Ghana by 2015. AGA was selected as a PR for the grant. The target was to protect 8 million people through IRS in the most endemic communities in Ghana. This would in-turn create over 3,800 jobs, build local capacity to sustain IRS, and strengthen partnerships for IRS provision across Ghana.

To support implementation, AGA implemented a range of risk mitigation systems and activities, including

- safety talks with attendance documentation,

- clear accountabilities and implications for safety breaches in any of its operations,

- ongoing risk reviews and

- a clear organizational process for risk reporting.

> *'Dividing up risks by national, zonal and district levels helps making risk management tangible. Mitigation systems need to be in place to make risk management work. An effective risk management system and tools are essential to achieve these goals.'* **Eric Obu Buetey, AGA**

AGA identified and categorized its major operational risks in programme implementation while, at the same time, identifying risk mitigation measures. These are shown in the table below:

**AGA risk management strategies**

| Risk | Risk Prevention and Mitigation |
|---|---|
| Limited program relevance, including inadequate baseline research on the | • Effective planning and implementation;<br>• Involving the relevant stakeholders in the implementation;<br>• Feedback/updates on |

| | |
|---|---|
| objectives of the programme and lack of interest on the part of relevant stakeholders to support implementation. | progress of work to stakeholders. |
| Inability to conduct or complete insecticide quality assessment by international QA specialists due to inadequate planning | • Timely and detailed planning of procurement systems, taking into consideration lead times, pre-shipment and destination sampling and testing;<br>• Consistent enforcement of GF Quality Assurance standards on IRS commodities;<br>• Batch testing of all insecticides procured and delivered to the programme; |

| | |
|---|---|
| | • Strict adherence to MSDS provided by the insecticide manufacturers and compliance with developed Standard Operational Procedures (SOPs). |
| Possibility of poor prescriber and provider adherence to internationally recognized diagnosis, treatment and prevention guidelines, patient's adherence to regimens, monitoring of adverse events, or other related of quality of | • Introduce a pharmacovigilance system into the program to promptly capture adverse events related to IRS at the community level;<br>• Batch testing/assessment of insecticides packages delivered onsite from suppliers;<br>• There are QA measures in place to mitigate poor quality spraying via monthly |

| | |
|---|---|
| health services and rational use of health products. | retraining programs, close supervision of small teams of spray men (4). |
| Delays in delivery of insecticide from manufacturers to end users (shipment, clearance at the port); no batch testing of insecticide conducted to ascertain the level of efficacy before using. | • Detailed planning and forecasting for insecticide requirement for each period leading to early ordering, shipment and delivery on site;<br>• Inventory control systems in place to provide stock level visibility on a weekly basis at the district, regional and national levels;<br>• Getting a dedicated team to oversee port clearance of program commodities. |

| | |
|---|---|
| Possibilities that Global Fund funded assets (non-cash) are lost due to theft or diversion by PR, SRs, other in-country partners or third parties. | • Periodic assets verification exercises in place to ascertain status of assets procured with grant and company funds;<br>• The procurement of fixed assets is done in line with delegation of authority document which is now fully in force;<br>• Internal and external audit controls mitigate this risk. There is also insurance cover for all company assets. |
| Introduction of new government policies, laws and levies/taxes without prior stakeholder consultation and | • High level engagement of government officials by GF/CCM to provide clarity on programme objectives and goals |

| | |
|---|---|
| input, leading to possible disruption of program implementation. | as well as grant conditionalities; <br> • Provision of periodic programme updates to high level government officials to keep them adequately informed about program implementation. |

**ENDA, Guinée-Bissau – Risk approach in a fragile state**

Environnement et développement du Tiers Monde (ENDA) works across the globe to support local efforts for environmental rehabilitation and preservation as well as for development. In Guinée-Bissau, ENDA support interventions addressing the complex circumstances of the country's HIV epidemic. This includes prevalence of multiple strains of HIV as well as high prevalence of HIV infection amongst women and specific key populations. ENDA programmes primarily target prevention of vertical transmission of HIV. There is very limited data on other modes of transmission in the country which restricts the development of targeted interventions for these populations. Finally, the country is situated in a region with ongoing political and civil conflict causing large movements of populations across borders.

*ENDA's risk management framework targets risks in three broad areas:*

- *Programmatic and performance risks;*

- *Financial and fiduciary risks; and*

- *Governance oversight and management risks.*

*Examples of major risks in each of these domains, as well as corresponding risk mitigation measures,* are shown in the table below:

**Programmatic and performance risks**

| Main Risks to achieving program objectives | Mitigation and Prevention Actions put in place |
|---|---|
| Data collected and processed manually | <ul><li>Reduction of deadlines for submission of reports to facilitate and improve data processing and quality assurance;</li><li>Implementation of SID, an electronic data and information system.</li></ul> |
| Not specific strategy for MARPs and | Ongoing negotiation with the PR based on ENDA's experience. |

| | |
|---|---|
| mobile populations | |
| Variety of tools to collect data not taking into account the specific indicators for all key populations. | Ongoing negotiation with the PR to harmonize tools. |
| Lack of integration of services (SRH / HIV) for PLWHIV, MARP and MARA (most at risk adolescents). | Lobbying with health system. |
| Certain health problems that occur in target populations (homosexuals, for example) are | Lobbying for inclusion of treatment and prevention of these conditions in the health system. |

| | |
|---|---|
| not taken into account in the health system. | |
| Lack of initiative and support for the improvement of services for MARPs and MARs | • Advocacy and lobbying with Civil Society Organization (CSOs) to take into consideration targeting of MARPs and MARAs in their workplans;<br>• Advocacy with UN women and UNOGBIS (Human Rights) for greater inclusion. |

## Financial and fiduciary risks

| Main Risks to achieving program objectives | Mitigation and Prevention Actions put in place |
|---|---|
| Diversity of accounting systems | Acquisition accounting software (SAGE) and provision of training to SRs and SSRs. |
| Multiplicities of SSR recipients (CBOs and government ministries) | • Contracts signed with the presence of a lawyer;<br>• Performance contracts signed with peer educators;<br>• Cash 0 policy (transport, per diem, supervision)'<br>• Payment based on results. |

## Governance, oversight and management risks

| Main Risks to achieving program objectives | Mitigation and Prevention Actions put in place |
|---|---|
| Quality of CCM members | Advocate with CSOs that are at CCM to have terms of reference for all CCM members. |
| Ongoing political instability | No effective actions can be taken. |
| Weak governance within CBOs | Capacity-building plan for CBOs |
| No ownership agreements with the Global Fund by the different Ministries which causes delays in the removal of products at the port. | Negotiation on a case by case exemption for needed products. |

ENDA has been working to improve the effectiveness of the CCM to identify and mitigate grant implementation risks. This includes

- promoting a diversity of CBO representation, including key populations;

- convening regular meetings with CBOs represented on the CCM;

- convening pre-CCM meetings to harmonize and exchange points of view on important issues to be addressed at CCM meetings; and

- implementing routine progress reports to the CCM and field visit plans.

# CHAPTER 6

## BUSINESS OBJECTIVES VS CURRENT REALITIES

Business objectives can be summarized into the following:

1. To meet a need or a set of needs
2. To make a profit
3. To continue in business

As an entrepreneur, you should periodically juxtapose these objectives with your current realities. You should periodically ask yourself the following questions and objectively answer them:

1. Is my business still meeting customers' needs?
2. What customer expectations have I not successfully met?

3. What can I do to meet these customer expectations?
4. Are my profits growing or declining or stagnated?
5. If profits are growing, what are the factors responsible for such growth?
6. If profits are declining or stagnated, what factors are responsible for such decline or stagnation?
7. What are the things that have the potential of ruining my business reputation?
8. Are there other factors threatening the continued existence of my business?

Objectively answering these questions will tell you if you will continue in business for the foreseeable future or not.

## INNOVATION IN BUSINESS

The entrepreneur must always remember that he operates in a dynamic business environment and therefore, cannot afford to be static or rigid in his approach as achieving his business objective is tied hugely to developments and changes in his business environment. He must keep himself continuously abreast with developments in his business environment in order to know the steps to take to tackle with the changes in his environment.

Every successful entrepreneur is known for his innovative abilities. They are known for their continuous development of business ideas and strategies on product and service improvements, customer satisfaction, cost reductions, profit maximization while not compromising quality of products and services delivery, and dealing with the competitions in their business environments ethically.

In a bid to achieve the set business objectives, the entrepreneur must continue to develop systems and create the environment that encourages the cultivation and implementation of new ideas to support internal processes and external business relations. Every member of the organization should be encouraged and trained to be innovative. In fact, the recruitment process should include sessions that will assess the innovative abilities of prospective employees.

Businesses that survive through time do so because of continuous service improvements, continuous product improvements, continuous process improvements, and continuous customer satisfaction. Businesses that do not survive with time are those that do not make continuous process and service improvements a major concern.

## CONCLUSION

Every entrepreneur (especially aspiring entrepreneurs) should ensure to research into businesses that have been involved in their type of business with a view to understanding why they succeeded or failed. If the entrepreneur is able to discover why they failed, he can set up systems to prevent his own business failure.

On the other hand, if he is able to discover the reason for the successes he sees, then he should work towards applying same principles and systems to ensure his own success.

**If you do what successful entrepreneurs did, you will get their type of success.**

## BIBLIOGRAPHY

1. STUDY.COM "what is business environment? – Definition, Factors & Quiz".
2. Businessdictionary.com
3. Investopedia.com
4. Investorwords.com
5. Wikipedia.org "Risk Management"
6. Solver.com/risk analysis "Risk Analysis – Overview"
7. Ourcommunity.com.au "Monitoring and reviewing risks in your organization"
8. Federal Highway Administration (FHWA) (2015) "Risk Assessment and Allocation for Highway Construction"
9. Sheppard, Ben, Melissa Janoske, and Brooke Liu. "Understanding Risk Communication Theory: A Guide for Emergency Managers and Communicators," Report to Human Factors/Behavioral Sciences Division,

Science and Technology Directorate, U.S. Department of Homeland Security. College Park, MD: START, 2012.

10. Africa CSO Risk Forum: Effective Risk Management for Successful Implementation of Programmes Supported by the Global Fund. December 5-6, 2013, Cape Town, South Africa

Summary Report of February 2014.